my soul feels lean

"Full of lived experience, Joyce Rupp shows how loss is the teacher and acceptance the friend that opens the door to 'peace with questions that have no answers.'"

Gunilla Norris
Author of *Simple Ways*

"In *My Soul Feels Lean*, Joyce Rupp offers us a key to the soul's deep places of loss and restoration. Open the door to her poetry and come on in; there will be rugged lands and flowering meadows—luring you into prayer and reflection."

Macrina Wiederkehr, O.S.B.
Author of *Seven Sacred Pauses*

"In the language of the soul, Joyce Rupp writes about the many faces of pain and grief in our lives. An honest, personal, and uncompromising look at the reality of loss and despair, which affects us all. Rupp takes us deeper into the journey with a powerful invitation to surrender to those moments of grace and healing that are available to us all in our darkest times. Authentic and deeply moving."

Edwina Gateley
Poet, Author, Speaker

JOYCE RUPP

my soul feels lean
poems of loss and restoration

Sorin Books  Notre Dame, Indiana www.sorinbooks.com

Paperback: ISBN-10 1-933495-56-1, ISBN-13 978-1-933495-56-9
E-book: ISBN-10 1-933495-57-X, ISBN-13 978-1-933495-57-6

Cover image © Thinkstock.com

Cover and text design by Brian C. Conley.

Printed and bound in the United States of America.

Library of Congress Cataloging-in-Publication Data
Rupp, Joyce.
  My soul feels lean : poems of loss and restoration / Joyce Rupp.
     pages cm
  ISBN 978-1-933495-56-9 (pbk.) -- ISBN 1-933495-56-1 (pbk.)
  1. Christian poetry, American. I. Title.
  PS3568.U65M9 2013
  811'.54--dc23

                          2012039796

To all those who have touched my life
with their kindness
and restored my hope

And when the day for my final voyage arrives,
and the ship, never to return, is set to leave,
you will find me on board, light on supplies,
and almost naked, like the children of the sea.

—Antonio Machado

Contents

Acknowledgments

These poems were created, edited, and reedited over many years. During that time a lot of people came in and out of my life. Numerous ones influenced the shape and voice of what I've written. While I cannot recall all their names, I am truly grateful for each individual who left an imprint on these pages.

There are some persons, though, whose names remain fresh within my realm of gratitude. Readers of my manuscript gave generously of their time to appraise and offer suggestions: Mary Kay Casey, Austin Repath, Art Schmidt, and Carmen Lampe Zeitler.

I found solitude for writing at the lakeside homes of Katie Bloom and Rose Roeder, at the monasteries of the Benedictines in Tucson, Arizona, and Fort Smith, Arkansas.

José Garcia brought his computer expertise to my office. Anthony Lee added his helpful assistance. Kathy Quinn gave her faithful help by contributing to the tasks I could not manage. My writing friends, Trish Herbert, Mary Kay

Shanley, and Macrina Wiederkehr, offered their much valued insights and support.

My community members, the Servants of Mary, cheered me on, as did the beloved members of the *Morning Midwives* weekly prayer and sharing group: Rebecca Kemble, Shelley Erickson, Mary Ferring, Joyce Hutchison, Mary Jones, Mary Mahoney, Kathy Quinn, Kathy Reardon, and Kathi Sircy. Janet Barnes and Frieda Molinelli never ceased praying for my needs. Pat Sloan Skinner continually introduced me to the work of her much loved poets. The Monday night poetry group at John and Carmen Zeitler's kept me immersed in verse.

The staff at Ave Maria Press/Sorin Books gave their gracious and attentive care in publishing my work. How fortunate I am to have had Robert Hamma's editorial recommendations and assistance as this book developed.

I also express my gratitude for Alice Meyers of Beaverdale Books in Des Moines, Iowa. She is one of those enthusiastic, steadfast supporters that every writer wishes to have.

My Soul

he asked me to write a poem
about my soul

my soul

I wondered how I could do that
without ample inspiration,
with only the mundane motive of presenting
my soul

I could tell of knowing my soul's songs
but that's not the same thing as writing about
my soul,
or is it?

I have felt my soul's surge of love
time and again, intuitively,

coming forth like a deep wave of the sea
washing through my wanting self
rising in the taste of solitary joy
sitting on the tongue of nature's beauty
laughing in the ear of my listening heart

but how do I write about this ephemeral
glimpse of goodness
that passes like a firefly through a summer's night?

how do I put into words
what I know of this essence, my being,

this eternal foundation
of all that is strong, true and worthy?

I believe
in soul, trust soul, follow soul's movements,
and love soul with all my being

maybe someday
words will show their face, as my soul does,
unexpectedly, lovingly,
but for now I'll simply be with

my soul

Loss

My soul was free and lean when I arrived at birth, having none of the encumbrances that quickly collected as I began to grow and develop. I soon learned, however, to hang on tightly to who and what I deemed to be of value. Wishes and wants gradually dominated my inner landscape. As much as I have tried to keep what I collected through these desires, life events continually divest me of some part of what I gain and hold tightly.

Now in my later years of life, I look at this process of loss and relinquishment and see its worth for my personal transformation. As I let go of what I hoped would be permanent, layer after layer of attachment is removed. My soul grows leaner and the view of who I truly am becomes clearer. I slowly regain that early freedom my soul had at birth, an ability to live more fully from my core of goodness. Now I can breathe love expansively and hold more lightly what I consider to be of greatest value.

I was well into my forties before I understood my reluctance to accept loss as a part of this refining and freeing process. When a former farm neighbor, Mrs. Staver, related an early life experience I'd forgotten, I had an "ah ha" moment. My family lived on a farm about a mile and a half from a small country church. Other buildings on the church property included the rectory, a three-room elementary school, and a small country store. Mrs. Staver told me how my family went to church one Sunday and stopped at the store afterward to buy a few items. In their hurry to get home they failed to notice I was missing among the brood of children and drove away without me. Summoning up my seven-year-old independence, I refused a ride from this neighbor and started to walk down the road toward home by myself.

As I thought about this event, my lifetime of goodbyes and losses took on a new perspective. I realized, for the first time, why I found farewells extremely difficult. Every significant goodbye held the secret agenda of being left behind by someone or something. I also discovered the source of my stubborn resiliency and dogged determination to move through challenging situations. Like that young child heading toward home, I managed to keep going on with my life, no matter what kind of loss occurred.

In spite of the clarity that came with knowing the root cause of my struggle with goodbyes, sometimes the truth of impermanence still leaves me wanting to run from them. Impermanence insists that *nothing* remains unchanged—loss is a natural occurrence in the flow of life. This reality implies the necessity and willingness to bid farewell to those who leave, to shed what no longer fits the shape of life, to let fall away those aspects of self that fail to enable growth, to skim off the details of the persona that keep one tethered to a false security.

My soul's leanness comes about through various sources of impermanence, many of them not of my preference or decision, such as the death of dear ones, changes in my physical demeanor, penetrating questions regarding my cherished beliefs, and upsets in human relationships. I do not want to have someone or something leave me without my choosing. Yet, no matter how much I appreciate a person, situation, or thing, my connection with each one will continually shift and alter. Whether I like it or not, loss is inevitable.

At some point in my personal development I recognized that not everything can be gained or controlled. Nor was control nearly as imperative as I once believed. Certain circumstances will continually chip away at my accumulated personal and spiritual possessions. I've learned that this impermanence is an evolving opportunity for transformation that will persist until the moment of physical death when only the treasure of love remains.

Experience has taught me that when life brings loss, I can either receive this situation openly or else clumsily trip over it by my resistant response. If I refuse to let go, my personal growth slows down. If I yield to the change being asked of me, grief-like emotions may still result, but their shape and quality will not be as severe because less energy is spent on resisting the change.

Accepting impermanence and entering into it without reluctance, self-pity, or gritty opposition comes about through recognizing the value and prerequisite of loss to deepen and strengthen my spirit. Letting go leads to inner freedom and harmony. Life becomes less of a potholed quandary and more a source of evenly placed contentment when I accept the loss of inner and outer treasures.

Eventually expanded insight comes when relinquishment is accepted. After each difficult loss and gradual acquiescence I am no longer quite as hindered by a need for ultimate security. Freed from another bit of inner encumbrance, my vision grows further beyond self to steadily embrace the larger world with care and compassion.

I see this in my own life as well as in others, particularly friends and those whom I serve as a spiritual companion. Each of us, in our own way, knows intuitively that we must enter fully into this process of loss and resultant growth if we are to mature. If we are open to the inevitability of relinquishment and give ourselves to what it requires of us, there will come a time when the uneven patterns of our existence become valuable sources of personal transformation.

A significant portion of my adult years has been spent absorbing this reality. I've given an even longer time to acknowledging the benefit of saying "yes" to what must be. Many of the poems in this section reflect this struggle in my life and in the lives of others I have known.

Finally I have come to understand that when I approach loss as my teacher, rather than my enemy, then it is that "the heart limps to the front door, tugs at the long-shut opening to the soul, and listens ("The Creaks and Cries of a Heart," p. 82). Then it is that I hear the deep resonance of peace that dwells within me.

My Soul Feels Lean

My soul feels lean,
trim, sparse,
excess and clutter
left behind,
desire and clutching
set aside.

And for the sake of what,
of what value
is this thinning,
weaning, letting go?

Only for the sake
of a clear eye,
an open mind,
an emptied heart.

All this, yes,
to enter
unencumbered
into oneness
with the One

where nothing
is everything.

Is Anything Left?

At the end of life
we look back and ponder,
look at what we thought we had
and realize it was so little.

We thought we knew, but now
we know we knew nothing.
We felt we were in charge
of the pieces of our life,
but now we see those pieces
strewn every which way.

We believed we had love
forever, but now that love
appears lost to us.
We hoped for a world
to give us happiness,
and now all that plenty
we aimed for spills
like water through an empty
sieve.

Is there anything left
as death nears?
Is there a morsel or two
in what we once held
as the fullness of life?

Not much. Not much left.

We go as we come,
from a safe womb
into unfamiliar terrain

where all we can bring
is our purified love
and empty, surrendered self.

You Wonder

You wonder
why you take those daily
steps, pushing
to get your work done,
to conform to a schedule
beyond accomplishment.

You wonder
when you end each day
with the discomfort
of not making the mark,
leaving much undone, unsaid,
unloved, unresolved.

You wonder
how you could miss
those moments of friendship,
those invitations to compassion,
those connections to a world
not of your making.

You wonder
if you could live life differently,
more in tune with your true self,
more in step with your deepest desires,
more in love with cosmic beauty,
more in sync with the world's desolate.

You wonder,
but then you continue forward
on the same old trek of dull
repetition, karmic garbage,
and sludgy unawareness.

Goodbye to Summer

Impermanence, transformation,
seasonal change, goodbyes.
Call it by whatever name,
its bound to leave a crusty mark
on my reluctant spirit.

The time has come to end
my light-filled summertime
when I floated on emerald wings.
Now I stand here by the patio door
looking out at naked trees.

Overnight, determined rain pressed
nearly every leaf to the ground.
Only a landscape of emptiness remains
where once there lived contented fullness.

I take a deep breath, give a sigh
of resignation, gather my precious
remembrance of those succulent months
while my memory takes one last, grateful look
at summer's dewy dawns.

Now is the time to yield, to enter
the next turning, accept the stark contrast
of barrenness in place of fullness.

As I turn away from the emptied trees
I take my generous basket of summer

with me, trusting it has stored
enough to see me through
until the time of melting snow.

I Lose Myself, Find My Self

I lose myself, find my self.
Consistently, unendingly.

With each finding I think,
"This is it, the last time,
now all is well."

Then it happens again.

Like now. I'm lost.
Yearning, searching
for the part of me
that carries peace.
The settled, happy self
that sings with the stars
and dreams with the moon.

But for now, I'm lost.
Walking through dim forests,
snagged by the underbrush,
moving through tangled days
in a fog, doing what must
be done. Trusting
I will find my self again.

Go toward That Which Repels

Rough terrain and jagged barbs
leave her doubting that the love
she desperately desires
will ever grow in her heart, in her deeds.

Thistles and thorns, thick briars,
her mind and heart
a wild hedge of judgments,
barriers to what love could be.

She wonders why she is lonely,
why the hollow canyon of her life
catches only brief slants of sunlight,
knows so few glimpses of green.

"Go toward that which repels,"
cries the deeper self.
"Accept limitations, move bravely,"
whispers the quiet voice of the soul.

Inner Freedom

she's ending her job,
walking away from years of work,
not even sure why
except that a strong voice inside
keeps urging her to do so.

it's the voice of freedom calling.
now that she has finally heeded it,
she's letting herself get manacled
in the chains of self-doubt and fear.

some people are always
putting themselves behind bars.

Leave Them Behind

Leave them behind.
Bid farewell to exaggerated emotions
dragging you down.
Let go of sharp-toothed thoughts
tempting you away from the face of love.
Cease judging the other unworthy
of your hysteric expectations.

Leave behind all
that harms, damages, or destroys
the delicate lotus blossom of love.

Open your heart to the good
flowing from the other.
Clear the mind to explore
what is of benefit.

No one contains all you want,
or need, or expect.

Katy and Theresa

They talk in low tones
giggle, whisper confidences,
enjoy one another's company
with a trusting, open love
many will never experience.

I lay on the navy blue futon
in the next room, reading
but also listening,
an envious ear turned
to where mother and daughter
lay in the apartment bed
before sleep enfolds them.

My mother and myself,
we shared many happy moments
but never were we so free,
never were we quite so content
as those two friends
snuggled in for the night
in the room next to me.

In this enviable moment
before turning off the light
I long for a return
of my beloved mother,
long to laugh with her,
to tell her secrets of my heart
without embarrassment or concern,

long to be at home with her
in the places of my soul
I regretfully kept to myself.

Refusal

She's in the desert, dying
of thirst; you offer her
life-giving water.
She turns away
scornfully.

She's in the wilderness,
starving to death. You offer her
nourishing food,
but she refuses it.

"It's okay for you to want that,"
she says vehemently, "you can believe it."
Then she gorges on self-pity
and old tears that only increase
her thirst and hunger.

You finally realize
you cannot force-feed her.
You cannot shove your experience
into someone else, no matter
how much you care.

You give up trying
to help.
You do the one thing,
the only thing you can.

You let go
and
simply love her.

Kenyan Thirst

A donkey rots in a river,
that same river
where buckets of water are drawn
to soothe parched throats
of empty-bellied people.

Children fade and die
from cholera
and the curable disease
of dehydration.

Babies suck on flaccid breasts
of mothers with despairing eyes.
Men with ribs like skeletons
dig determinedly through dry graves of sand,
begging the land to yield it's treasure
from the water table
far, far below.

And I, I go to the faucet,
rinse my glass, toss the life-saving liquid
down the drain,
fill the glass to the brim again
and drink beyond my thirst.

Coveted Growth

When one flower somewhere,
anywhere,
garden, roadside, meadow, forest,
opens her first blossoms,
do other flowers bend their hearts
with resentment, envy, hostility,
jealously coveting those blooms
hearkening to sun and sky?

Do they wrench inside
and push their unready buds
into an anxious race
toward fulfillment?

Or is this something only
humans do
in their need to win a race
never meant to be won?

Helpless

"Helpless." Her word
for how she feels as she watches
her beloved spouse
slip away,
breath by breath, day by day,
weaker and less able to walk, talk, eat.

"If only we knew," she explains,
"then we'd have a focus. We could
deal with the illness."

But they do not know the cause
of the insistent malady, the ogre
stealing his strength,
robbing his body of its vitality.

Faithfulness becomes the norm,
years of love binding them
one to another. She wakes him,
guides him to the kitchen.

Together they share the meal,
slowly, silently. She wonders
how long before this is the last time
there will be a walk to the table.

The only medicine now is of the heart,
the marrow of love,
the only thing giving these two
a purpose to continue.

Love So Easily Gets Lost

love so easily
gets lost
in the winding caverns
of the distracted heart,

pushed to the far corners,
forgotten
in the rush and run
of everyday stress,

ignored in the folly
of anger, rigidity, disdain,
unattended in the fog
of depression and desolation.

love waits without whining,
stands tall and strong
in the prison of forgetfulness,
waits to be released.

love needs more than
a valentine's paper message,
more than a hurried hello.

love longs to be called forth
from the heart's hiddenness,
yearns for faithful attention,
uncluttered awareness.

listen, hear the stirring
within, reach to where love
eternally resides.

call love out
from the deep recesses.
embrace
what is so easily lost
in a fragile, uncertain world.

The Terrorist

The threat of terrorism
looms daily
from the headlines,
news anchors reporting
violent deeds, bloody deaths.

In my illusory cocoon
of safety, I move confidently,
unaware of danger lurking
in the domain of my very self,

the terrorist inside,
pressing my face
into the hard ground
of my calendar, endless tasks,
duties and must-be-dones.

The terrorist inside
sneaking behind the wall
of my supposed compassion,
gunning down the innocent
with judgmental thoughts
and harsh, emotional responses.

The terrorist inside,
bombing verbally
those who get in the way
of my ego-pronouncements
and vindictive desires.

The Death of Friendship

Friendships, ripened ones,
some pure as crystal glass,
offer the red wine
of supportive presence.

Other friendships, just as aged,
gradually hold a quiet boredom
grown weak and cloudy
from habitual neglect.

These dying friendships might merit
resurrection
but most often they fade into
the cellar of dullness.

Forgotten are the years
of bonding and enjoyment,
forgotten, too, the reasons
why this friendship
stirred and grew.

Left are the empty grapevines
of a now defunct connection,
memories not strong enough
to bring back what once held
juice and joy.

Rhonda

Rhonda smells of cigarettes
and never stops complaining.
Woe to the hapless visitor
who invades her hospice room,
chastised by an irritated voice
as thin and frail as her nicotine skin.

While death stares out
from the closet
she propels her silent fears
and heavily masked struggles
through doors of manipulation
and the cracked, dry walls
of her bitchy commands.

There are a million ways to die
and this is one of them.

She Feels Old at Twenty-Eight

She feels old at twenty-eight,
her fear of never marrying
a black claw scratching
last chance in her mind
every time she meets a possible
Mr. Love.

She can't trust that part of her self,
the radiant soul of godly stock,
to preserve its inherent texture
without a life-line to another.

The power of loneliness
drowns the inner voice
assuring her she is enough.

Falling in love, being in love,
finding a partner, being married,
all this, holy and blessed,

but until the black claw
is withdrawn and peace with self
gathers into acceptance,
another person only distracts
from what the heart already
possesses.

Airport

I sit here studying
round, square, long faces,
tall, lean, wide bodies,
the shape
of humanity in its many forms
and languages.

Every passenger seated here
going somewhere.

Each of us considers our life
unique, individual, lasting,
but soon this life
we consider vital and enduring
will be over. They pass by me now
and I see death in each one:
there sits cancer of the breast,
there goes heart attack, there stands
car accident and leukemia.
There walks congestive heart failure,
diabetes, AIDS.

Swiftly, with every heartbeat,
our lives move toward an end.
Yet while we wait or hurry
in the airport of life
we think this life, MY life, is essential
and immortal.

The Screaming

The screaming inside
never stops;
anger and fear
keep her forever held
in the crib of victimhood.

She rises only long enough
to condemn her illusions,
to foist her verbal spittle
upon the inner enemies
who trample on her identity
and personal worth.

Self-sabotaged time and again,
paranoid, suicidal,
raging against the walls
she builds around herself,
daily she weakens,
wobbling toward destruction.

What can I do,
as guide and companion,
to lessen her pain?

How can I nurture
a soul immersed
in her obsessive agony?

I listen with kindness,
respond with compassion,
offer encouragement toward
growth.

But this illness defies
the healing
I propose.

Greedy for Too Many Things

ravenous for too many things,
even spiritual growth,
greedy to grow without effort,
to have it all, to sit back and bask,
luxuriating in what was never mine
in the first place.

greedy for more time in the day
when I already have
all the time I need.

greedy for companionship
while I ignore the One Companion
always near.

greedy for, oh, so much,

while I miss the chipmunk
chewing on the sunflower seed,
the sound of soft July wind
rustling cottonwood leaves,
the color of azure sky as the sun
rinses morning out of it.

Saying All the Wrong Things

some days I feel like
I say all the wrong things
at the wrong time

words romp out
of a mouth that never stops
my tongue takes over
in marathon looseness
while my brain
idles away the day
in a trough of unawareness

doing verbal damage
making thoughtless statements
giving inane comments
spoken by the queen of egoism
and the jester of foolishness

when the day ends
I sweep up the verbal damage
aghast at what I see
in the commentary of disgust

holding this in full view
I wonder what ancient creature
crept inside my vocal chords
to stomp haphazardly
on unsuspecting souls
and spit upon the undeserved

Mistaken Perceptions

She pretends to seek advice
but rarely accepts it.
The trickles of her paranoia
form puddles, then creeks,
now a river in her brain.
Whenever her expectations
are not met, she builds a wall
brick
by
brick
until each friend
turns into an enemy,
each word
and deed
another reason
to stockpile supplies
behind the thick fortification
of her mistaken perceptions.

The Strongest Friendship

The strongest friendship
on a bad day
can be marred,
scarred with a foul mood
belching leftovers
from shadowed disagreements
never fully digested.

Beware of all that growls
in the belly of irritation.
Dodge the gurgle of thoughtless
language, words that sour
in remembrance,
responses that lodge so deeply
they will forever cause reflux.

Avoid narcissistic binges.
Hold back the freedom
to speak whatever the gut
regurgitates.
Breathe silently into love
lest the foundation of many years
be torn apart and vomited
by a few careless comments.

"Please forgive me"
never fully quiets the upset.
The bad taste in the mouth
of injured friendship
keeps coming back,
setting off endless heart-burn.

Wealthy Woman

Wealthy woman in a rich land
watches a documentary
on war refugees from Sierra Leone,

views matcheted limbs, skinny people
with hands and arms missing,
tents filled with homeless families,
children who have known
nothing but war, hunger, grime.
They wait for when they can go
back home.

To what? Not to the clean, largess
living of the comfortably prosperous,
not to supermarkets bulging
with options, not to paved streets
and schools with books for children.

They go back to poverty, to empty
streets, empty stores, empty shacks,
empty land.

And the wealthy woman in a rich land,
she watches, moved for an hour or so,
a pricking of guilt from the sharp needle
of awareness piercing the skin of her oblivion.

Then she goes on living with her closet
full of clothes, her shopping cart heaped

with the carnage of abundance, her life
replete with attainable distractions,

and forgets what she has seen.

Palm Sunday

Three men
proclaiming the memory
of your path to Calvary.
Three men
with somber voices
making all the appropriate
pauses and inflections.

But what I remember
is the Calvary
beside me,
the man
whose body odor
invaded my space,
the man
seemingly homeless,
surely mentally challenged.

The three men
went on and on and on
with their words
telling the history
of your suffering.

I found you
not in their stiff words
but next to me,
a man still bearing
the heavy cross
of loneliness and rejection.

The Lone Evening Star

As I went to pull the window shade
the lone evening star last night
called strongly to my busy heart:
"Look! Look! Come back
and vigil with me."
I thought I would. I meant
to do so, later in the evening.
But I stayed instead with work
and went to bed
without a second nod
to the one who waited
all night for me.

Blue Jay Heart

There's a lot of squawk
And noise
In my blue jay heart

Too much loud anxiety,
Endless clamoring
Of things yet to be accomplished

I land on a branch
Of stillness
Only long enough
To catch my scattered disturbances

Then I quickly fly forth
Into the web of life
With a raucous cry
Of activity

Slashing the peaceful air
With a voice
Of scolding urgency

The Old Cottonwood

The old cottonwood
has long ago shed his bark.
Pale skin of the thick trunk,
aged flesh grown translucent
is all that remains.

With only a few sparse branches
left to keep him company
he bends over the forest floor
almost horizontal in posture,
bowing to the azure sky.

I expect with each strong wind
to find him lying flat on his stomach,
but, no, his journey to death
is a slow diminishment,

not unlike the bodies I see
still alive with unhurried death
in the Pleasant Valley nursing home,
the strong roots of their years
holding them, too, in this world,
as deeply as the old cottonwood
veering toward annihilation.

These Gray Winter Days

These gray winter days linger
    like dormant moles.
The shortest days of light are upon us
    and I feel their pull
drawing me toward an invisible cave
    where sleep prevails.
Sunshine lies somewhere in memory,
    but nowhere in this land.
Only the dull scrape of snow shovels
    scratching the sidewalks of boredom,
while the eternally ashen curtain
    descends with determination.

Sensing my own need for dormancy
I accede to the gray wintertime
and turn toward my cave of incubation.

Azalea Leaves

light raindrops
    rinse the tired azalea leaves

slowly washing off
    the dreary residue
    of a hot summer's glaze

not enough moisture
    to reach
    the parched roots

but every droplet
    cheers the slaked plant,
    reminding it of better days
    when rain fell steadily

when there was no need to cry out
    for nurture, for comfort,
    for relief

the azalea in me
    remembers my own dry years
    of waiting and wanting,
    the parched yearning
    of my desolate spirit

when the least measure
    of relief
    kept me from the death
    of joy

from what seemed to be
an infinite desert
of unhappiness.

Pinnacles of Winter

Pinnacles of translucent winter
hang from the cottage roof,

fierce as untouchable swords,
strong enough to slice off a hand,
daring anyone to cling
for more than a momentary touch.

They patter steadily on the wet ledge,
their strength melting in the January sunshine,
surrendering themselves to annihilation
like a weathered crone sighing love songs
on her death bed.

April Goldfinches

Goldfinches gather at the feeder,
golden odes of sparkling spring,
their freshly molted feathers
aglow in the morning sunshine.

I watch the finches with an eye
of pleasure
but my heart holds stale tears.

A tethered hurt refuses to fall
from my gathered memories.
This month, this anniversary,
they all come forth again,

the finding on the floor, the long
wait in the emergency room,
two days of bedside vigil,
the final wisp of breath gone,
the word "never" rooted like stone
in the temple of my heartache.

So while the goldfinches fly into spring
with their airy, yellow brightness,
the unshed tears of death press
against each other,
refusing to depart my mournful heart.

Will I ever be done with this grief?
Will the sadness inside ever molt itself
into acceptance?

Every April, every anniversary,
I wonder if this be the springtime,
if this be the year,
when my wintered feathers
complete their molting into gold.

One Lone Goose

One lone goose came
from the west,
flew into the fresh daylight
of the east,
honked as he circled
above me
and then turned back
to meet the western sky.

I stood on the sidewalk
and gazed,
believing some message
had been sent,
undecipherable
but definitely there.

I wondered what it was
that brought that lone goose
to circle above me
in the light of dawn.

"Wake up," were the only
words arising, a call perhaps
to fuller attention,

but deep down I knew
there was something more
trailing from that lone goose
to my veiled heart.

That solitary creature,
coming from the place of darkness
moving to the place of light
and circling back again,

configured the round
of existence. I did not know then
how it spoke to me of death
and its completeness.

Three months later
my soul-friend died,

and then I knew.

Ninety Years

she bent her still agile frame
of ninety years,
pulled two dusty trays
from the bottom cupboard shelf,
stirred the huge kettle
of fresh chicken broth,
tossed the broken leaves of romaine lettuce
with her favorite thousand island dressing,
whacked off two fat drumsticks
from the full bodied chicken,
knifed the moist meat
onto small luncheon plates,
spooned the clear broth into cups,
scurried around and found
two unwrinkled paper napkins.

together we carried the trays
full of food, prepared with joy
and her endless relish for life,
into the cozy sun room
where we dined amid happy conversation.

I knew that day
a strange, uneasy humility,
the act of being waited upon
by someone much older and less able
than myself.

I felt that day
excruciating discomfort, reluctance,
as I bent back my independence,
withdrew my capable strength
and accepted the challenge of needing
only to receive.

Death Invades My Days

Death invades my days,
sifts through the filters
of my life,
straining out the strongholds
of self importance,
leaving only the bare portions
of lasting love.

Death sweeps in boldly,
calling itself Parkinson,
ovarian cancer, leukemia,
heart attack and old age,

wearing the face of a mother,
a cousin, a brother, a niece,
a husband, a father, a friend.

Some whom death snatches
I know intimately, others
barely at all, but each
death strains out what I have grasped,
separates what I thought
I had to have.

I look into the sieve of my life
and see now how little
I really need.

Crushing Coincidences

A day for a picnic in the park,
simple joys, easy happiness,
above them a nine foot tree branch
falls at that very moment,
crushing a woman
whose head only moments before
filled with laughter.

A day like any other day,
a man walks hurriedly to work,
a noise, the careening of a car
into a taxi passing by,
the taxi smashes a fire hydrant
whose forceful water gushes out
crushing the man walking near it.

A day of innocent camaraderie,
school is over and the small group
of chattering high school girls
crosses a familiar street.
One girl's scarf falls to the ground.
She reaches quickly to pick it up
in front of an oncoming truck
that crushes her young life.

If only each one had been
one minute later,
or earlier,

but death chose its own day,
leaving the whys and what ifs
to float through the hazy sky.

My Fear of Losing You

Beneath our enduring friendship
the unspoken, latent fear
I never mentioned to you,
that I would lose you
to work, to poor health,
to a faraway move
or something unforeseen.

And then one day I did lose you.

Death sliced you from me
with a condor's swiftness,
ripped you out of
my fearful grasp without
a moment's hesitation.

Always death wins
in who gets to keep.

You are gone now
and so is my old fear,
leaving plenty of room
for loneliness and sorrow

but also sufficient space
for the savoring of love,

the one thing Death
could not take from me.

Margaret

What anguish your gentle body knew
in the final months before departure.
Those fierce blood clots blackening your feet,
creeping through your limbs, deadly dark.
The surgeon finally cutting, sawing, suturing,
leaving you with stumps aching for wholeness.

All through those weeks of raw pain
you submitted, yielded, surrendered
with faith and courage. You became
a mentor of how one enters agonizing death.

On my first hospital visit you said to me,
"I wonder what my mother would think of this."
When you spoke those words I knew
you were not long for this realm of life,
thoughts and words of ancestors bringing
another layer of existence intimately close.

On my last visit to the hospital you held
my hand,
looked serene and calm,
love in your eyes and peace in your words
even though your emptied torso
obliterated all hope of ever carrying you
on your own.
We both knew without saying it
that death was determined to have its way.

You left us on an early Sunday morning
when the night still held thick layers of dark.

Margaret, was your mother there to hold you,
to welcome you as a newborn
to the place of peace?
I trust you found your limbs again
and danced with joy.

He's Burying His Mother Today

He's burying his mother
on his sixtieth birthday,
she who once held his fresh body
wet from her silken womb.

Now he walks on the dry soil
as he goes to say a final farewell
to the woman who liberated him
into the life that has been his.
It is she who has now been freed.

There is no graveside gushing blood,
no painful contractions, no rending
of a full womb, for this woman went peacefully
at age ninety-seven, just up and left
between sips of soup at the nursing home,
looked up, smiled, and was gone.

He stands by the deep hole
ready to entomb his mother's body
while a heavy cord of ache
quietly unravels in the far corner of his heart,
sensing an unnamed awareness
of that long umbilical cord of love
that death threatens to sever.

He sees himself in her warm lap,
remembers his early years of play
and the later ones of her encouragement
while he wandered into his true self.

He doesn't wish her back here
knowing she was ready to leave,
and yet, as he moves from the graveside
and slowly walks to the waiting car
a large tear threads down his cheek.
For he senses a final goodbye,
how he is losing something
of those honey suckled months
in his mother's womb,
and the years that grew beyond them.

On the Death of Sister Flavia

Inch by inch we dwindle,
one by one we die.
The great ones have gone,
the valiant who prepared the way,
the prophets who demanded we grow,
the nurturers who tended our roots,
the maimed of heart and mind
who never did get well.

All of them are going.

Step by step they slip to their graves
leaving us their legacy,
bequeathing us their wisdom
while we huddle in the sighing circle
of uncertainty.

Flat markers increase in the cemetery,
empty pews vigil in the chapel,
fewer tables sit in the dining room.

Our community sucks in a breath
while the circle of kept tears
rocks in denial and false hope.

One by one we become smaller.
Is it only a matter of time
before we all fall flat
and the vacant circle
is swallowed by the wind?

Will the vision of the founders go blind?
Will the ancestry's wisdom perish?
Will the vulture of demise descend
upon the last of us?

Evangelista

Evangelista, my elderly friend,
a wise woman whose insight
and easy humor stretched me
beyond my youthful perceptions.

Now she's a different person.

One lousy cerebral stroke
has stolen her gentle voice
and captured her creaky limbs.
Soon, it will rob her totally.

Today her thin, frail body
lies motionless on a hospital bed,
IV tube connecting her to fluids
while she dreams the dark sleep
none of us can enter.

I call her name quietly
and welcome the surprising smile
that slides out of her deep slumber,
overjoyed at seeing momentary light
in her grey-blue eyes.
I glimpse for one brief space
the woman she has been,
the one I have loved and admired
for so long.

Soon she surrenders once more
to a place beyond that refuses my visitation.
Little lines of clear drool slip
from the corners of her wrinkled mouth,
her raggedy-doll head lopping over,
a vibrant spirit ebbing from an aged body.

As I sit there sadly musing at what must be
I whisper "Go home" to her imprisoned spirit,
but this body of hers does not listen to me.

After one hundred years of faithfully
housing a soul,
it is not yet ready.

Grandfather

They're keeping him alive,
those two tiny infants
floating closely in the womb,
twin girls imbibing
from a daughter-in-law's life,
the first and only third generation
his eyes will ever see.

The immensity of his love gathers
toward the goal,
pushes him into daily endurance
armored with deadly chemotherapy
draining endlessly into tired veins.

Days of exhausted immobility,
months of listless waiting,
more rounds of powerful chemicals
to hold the voracious cancer at bay.

His thoughts linger fondly
on these children, *his* grandchildren.
Always in his heart: "The twins,
The twins. I will live to see the twins."

Not long before death arrives
two healthy granddaughters declare
their song of life for the first time.
A thousand or so miles away
the dying grandfather is given a first look.

He beams with gratitude at the small faces
coming to him on the computer screen,
imagines their birthing cry, their soft touch,
his ashen face flooding with love.

Now he has seen.
Now he can go.
And he does.

Christina

The nurse wheels her frail body
into the dining room;
there, a small semblance
of a former self dissolved within
the skewed patterns
of dementia and Alzheimer's.

Speech left her some months ago,
now she eats only when food
is brought to her hesitant mouth.

Where has her former self gone,
the warmth, the laughter, the generous
interest in others, all those gracious qualities,
where are they now?

I sit beside her, feeling privileged to hold
the spoon of applesauce to her mouth,
to lift the glass of water carefully to her lips,
my free hand lightly touching
her bony shoulder
now divested of its fleshy softness.

As I prepare to leave, I bend over
to kiss her painfully hollow cheek.
She lifts her head upward, looks at me,
a slow smile forms, and then, a miracle!

She speaks

of mother and father, her family and mine,
the closeness we had, memories jumbled
and somewhat incoherent, yet spoken with joy
in her voice and words of gratitude.

Somewhere, underneath Christina's
winding thread of words,
her strong affection assures me
she has not yet left
after all.

Aileen

You have entered the Great Silence,
taken wing at a moment's notice,
leaving those who treasure you
here among a world of words
that fail to satisfy our loss.

You have joined the Sacred Oneness,
slipping easily into the curve
of complete unity, leaving us behind
in the world of complexity.

You have eased into the Blessed Peace,
tossing aside human concerns,
moving beyond hidden things of the mind
that trouble and taunt serenity.

You have united with the One Love,
holding within you your gentle affection
for those who grieve your departure,
gathering these loves into the Forever Love.

You have arrived at the Eternal Realm
waiting for us, gone into the distance
to dwell in Endless Abundance,
to drink from the Chalice of Eternity.

We yearn for your presence
while we remain here, waiting
until it is our turn to slip away
into the cradle of Honored Mystery

where we, too, enter the Great Silence,
and words no longer craft our destiny.

After the Funeral

They've gone now,
all of them. The faces
whose eyes
shimmered with tears
equal to hers,

the caring embraces
momentarily
easing the hollowness
of loss,

the words of comfort
given with kindness,
the stories told
with hope of gathering the past
into a vault of treasures.

They've gone,
all of them.

And she is alone
with her loneliness,

left with an enormous shaft
of emptiness,
space that once held
the beloved constancy
of presence.

She turns slowly toward
the rest of her life, wondering,
"What shall I do? What shall I do
now that they've gone?"

Grief Has Come to My House

Grief has come to my house,
entered without invitation,
banged on my locked door,
slashed the tightly fitted screens,
smashed in the durable windows.

She sits now in my heart's best chair,
staring at me with bleeding eyes,
cobwebs of sorrow in her hair,
clumps of sadness on her sour breath.

Grief, my unwelcome visitor,
demands constant attention,
cleans out my well-stocked pantry,
gobbles up my daily energy,
and refuses to give me any sign
of imminent departure.

I have unlocked the door now
but she never goes near it.
In spite of listening to her endless pain
and brushing away her constant tears,
she still clings insistently to me,
refusing to walk out of my life.

What more does she expect,
surely not my friendship?

Anger

I turned my face to Anger,
told him to stop charging in
each time a new pain visits,
chided him for his endless greed
every time my life gets unhinged,

but he only stood there defiantly,
reading off the list of the dead,
coughing up the phlegm of memories,
enumerating my aching wounds,

all the while fiddling around
with his plump fingers
on the ripped and ragged edges
of my broken heart.

You Keep Your Sorrow

You keep your sorrow to yourself
not because you want to hoard it;
there is only so much of your sadness
someone else can perceive and absorb.

Grief is a lonely task, done
ultimately in the tearful cove
of the human heart, cried out
in the vast emptiness
of wordless days, sleepless nights.

Oh, you talk to others about your pain,
and if you are brave you even speak
of tears and more tears,
but there's only so much another
wants to hear, tries to hear,
will hear, can hear.

When grief continues to gnaw
on the bones of goodbye,
month after month and on into
the next year, and maybe the year
after that, no one wants to know
about your desolation and sharp stabs
of loneliness.

They want you to be *happy*
but *happy* can't be had,
so you keep your sadness to yourself

where it sits in a leaden mine
of heartache
a thousand feet deep inside of you.

Uncontrolled Grief

never think you can control
grief,
never imagine that now, finally,
you have her figured out
or left her wet web
of sadness behind you.

never think for a moment
that the last piece of loss
has surfaced and been shed.

for just when you are sure
grief has departed,
she comes again with
her persistent sorrow,

another sweeping away
of recovered joy,
another abandonment
of restored energy.

once more the heart plummets
into mourning,
waits for the slow footsteps of hope
to re-emerge,

humbled by grief's strength,
readied once more
to succumb
to what must be
and is.

Taste the Sadness

Taste the sadness.
Bring the full cup
to the lips of your heart.
Imbibe slowly
for it is fetid and bitter.

Taste the pain.
Bring the full cup
to the mouth that resists.
Drink deeply
for it seeks acceptance.

Pour your grief
into the vacant canyon
of your love.
Let it circulate
among the deadness.

Let the sadness ferment
in the vat
of your homeless soul.

Let it be. Let it be.

Someday, fine wine.
Today, only sadness.

Falling

falling falling falling
falling
apart

a leaf gone adrift
an acorn bouncing on a roof
a twig torn from the branch
falling falling falling

no one notices
except me

inside
splinters of broken glass
stones tumbling from a hill
pieces of a puzzle strewn
threads loose
unraveling endlessly
falling falling falling

they all think
I will never fall apart
what they do not know
is that I am already
falling falling falling

careening into fractures
collapsing into pieces
dropping into splotches
shredding into slices

falling falling falling
falling
apart

The Creaks and Cries of a Heart

. . . the creaks and cries of a heart slowly opening.
—Florida Scott-Maxwell

It doesn't happen in a day.
The heart slowly closes the door,
disenchanted with people, work, God,
refusing to let in more confusion,
slamming the door shut on sorrow,
pulling the shade down on challenge,
hiding out from the carnage of rejection.

The process of petrifaction
crawls slowly into the cells of love,
squeezing out the last remnants of joy,
hardening the arteries of tenderness,
compressing the atoms of enthusiasm.

Gradually all relationships taste flat,
work reeks of boredom or struggle.
God takes up residence in another house,
and food, drugs, drink
dull the memory of the soul's singing.

But the soul of love is persistent.
She finds our address in the dumpster,
begins the hungry hunt for home
and lays siege to our barriered heart
with a constant "come out! come out!"

In spite of our deadness, we hear.
We fight, we hide, we tremble.
The covers come up over our heads.
We sneak behind busyness, illness,
refusing to yield to the loving voice,
the one demanding a return to life.

All day and night, especially at night
in wild dreams that toss us deeper,
the voice harangues, "come out!
I know you're in there. Come out!"

Finally the heart limps to the front door,
tugs at the long-shut opening to the soul,
and listens.

Restoration

One day in late November I was coming back from a walk along Saylorville Lake. The wild wind that day ripped through the cool air as I made my way up a steep, clay-encrusted embankment. There I found a narrow path through a thick patch of dried weeds that the wind bounced and shoved toward me. Sticky sand burrs caught on my pants legs and shoestrings. Emptied seedpods on tall brown stems poked their scratchy faces into mine. As I moved up the hill I stopped and marveled how, in the midst of a dying season, there was already movement toward rebirth. The burrs were eager to travel any place they could find a resting spot and begin anew in the spring. The same with the seedpods. They had flung their occupants to the ground, trusting the winter snows would protect them until April rain and sunshine drew them into green.

Such is the way with the natural world. And such is the way with the human world, too, if only we will believe it. Restoration and revitalization of some form follows our time of loss if we allow ourselves to engage in the required letting go. We won't be able to reestablish what we once had but we will receive some new seed of growth to take us further on the road of personal transformation.

Even though there are times when new growth is elusive and the current situation is grim, I have long been a person of hope. No matter how much loss invades my days and nights, I remain turned toward the possibility of some kind of renewal following leave-taking. This positive attitude comes from my early farm life where I watched seasons of the earth turn naturally from one to another, leaving fruitfulness behind for emptiness, emptiness behind for fruitfulness. My hope also arises from a personal faith grounded in the Christian belief of life-death-resurrection.

Along with these two foundational sources, the insight and clarity of purpose I receive when the pain of loss finally abates also confirms my hope. Loss has taught me to live in the present, instead of clutching the past or grasping at the future. Loss has encouraged me to find joy and meaning *here* instead of pining for it elsewhere, to live more simply and be content with less, to appreciate more fully what I now have. I've gained a keener appreciation for the significant people in my life and learned to not take them for granted. Probably no gift has been greater in my own situation than that of compassion. Each emptying and letting go has brought a keener awareness of how others also suffer loss in some way.

Observing the revitalization of life around me, whether in the form of nature or people, restores my belief in future growth when loss dominates my life. I see how others maintain their ability to rise from the ashes. The return of migrating birds in spring increases this assurance, as do numerous other insights from nature. Something so simple as a little frog in a pond can restore my inner balance if I am willing to slow down long enough to observe the frog, and not run quickly to the next thing on my schedule.

I find that intentionally easing the fast pace of my days is indispensable if a spirit of hope is to be sustained in tough times. Being overly active and involved in the constant bombardment of social media or other stress-induced activities whittles away my ability to go to the deeper places of life. Without daily attention to what lies beyond the outer world I can easily get mired in the non-essentials and miss the hidden movement leading to future maturity.

Winter, the season that many people abhor or put up with, has actually assisted me in accepting the pain of loss and in trusting the restoration of hope. Winter brings with it a lessening of activity in order for the soil and vegetation to rest and recover needed strength. This fallowness provides for the regeneration of the natural world's vitality. The increase of darkness and the lessening of light-filled days extends an invitation to enter slowness within myself, to approach it positively. Like winter, this gestating period gives me an opportunity to restore my inner strength and enthusiasm for life.

Years of knowing both loss and restoration have assured me: after letting go, I can move forward. There awaits something of worth even though I may feel emptied and forsaken, beaten or humbled by loss. The truth of how little I need to be happy grows in me.

The cycle of loss and restoration strengthens my belief that each of us can learn how to "surrender to the soul's ripening" and open our heart "to how love calls" ("Live This Day," p. 156).

I Hear Spring Breathing

I hear Spring breathing softly,
her quiet respiration
rising and falling
through the heavy snow banks
gurgling in the sunshine.

I hear the slow, steady intake
of mid-February air
stirring the awakening crocus.

I hear the sigh
of the oak tree's terminal buds,
warm wind stretching them out
beneath the turquoise sky.

I hear my own lungs
inhaling and exhaling
with renewed hope,
ready for the coming
of green and the shedding
of all that is grayed
with winter's feigned death.

Surprising Surrender

a solitary, white-haired woman
on the morning of her sixty-first birthday,
coffee in hand, rests by an expansive lake.
she sits at the rim
of the waters calling to her opened soul.

the silvery dancing steps
of the alive morning sun
slip across the ever shifting waves,
drawing her into their easy rhythm.

a symphony of light playing
on the crested water
lures her with its splendor
and she forgets for a moment
her longing for things yet to be,
so overcome is she by the silvery dance
carrying her
into the re-birthing hands
of beauty.

gratitude for the glimpse of fullness
in the sparkling splendor
overtakes her, and in that moment
she ceases to clutch her concerns
of unmet satisfaction,

content now to join the dance of eternity
within her silent self,
willingly wooed into surprising surrender.

Light in the Eyes of the Dying

all of them women
all of them dying
all of them shining

Nancy was the first.
I did not realize the Light then,
only saw this glow in her,
softening her entire being.

Jeanne was next.
ah, that day at the hospital
sitting on the edge of her bed,
she smiled at me
and a thousand stars
glimmered in her hollow eyes.

Evelyn Barbara followed.
only a spider-like skeleton
left of a once sturdy woman,
yet the Light emanating from her
is something I shall not forget.

then there was Leanna.
I can't recall the day
the Light grew large in her,
but it was there.
I felt it strongly in that final embrace,
a candle burning intensely between us
as I leaned into the fullness of her arms

how does the Light become stronger,
how does it grow more intensely
as the going gets closer?
this I ponder and find no answer,
but I know it to be true.

For a Brief Moment

for a brief moment
early spring rain ceases.
the sun breaks through
grey sky.

threads of gold,
thin enough to pierce
the forest,
glitter on dewdrops,
touching the eyelashes
of blooming forsythia,

making of the yellowed bushes
a place where beauty
bows to brilliance,

where everything arrogant
takes off its shoes
to stand on holy ground.

New Zealand Rainforest

Surrendered nobility
rests quietly
on the leafy woodland floor.

Giant trunks of ancient trees
have plummeted
from their secure height
to the graveyard of decay,

giving themselves
to the summons of death
without seeming reluctance.

Somewhere in their limbs
they carry the secret
that death never has the last word.

I see on their decaying bodies
tender moss, sturdy lichen, emerald fern
and other rich inhabitants
homing their way into life,
gestated and nourished by the fallen limbs.

I walk within the corridors
of this early morning,
sensing kinship with earth's eastering,

finding hope, hearing its
quiet song, feeling

a steady rhythm of life
beating among the dead
here
in the New Zealand rainforest.

Franklin Gulls

A field full of dark,
opened earth
freshly turned to the spring air,
a flock of Franklin gulls,
pure white wings,
angelic images on black soil,
hungry birds searching
for a mouthful of sustenance.

I pause before this scene
to see the luscious lips of earth
welcoming the invaders,
beckoning them to taste
what lies within
the thick folds of darkness.

New Year's Day

The structured frame of a year,
my culture's way of marking
the spaces, the lived moments
of my existence,

but does anything really change
with the coming of a new year?

The same sun rose in the east.
People yawned and grunted
the same way they always do,
the same loves, the same quarrels,
the same stuck points, the same
attitudes toward war and peace.

So why did my morning heart
tingle with hope as I arose,
as I walked silently among
the same woods, on the same path?
Why did this same heart quietly fill
with a strong response of gratitude?

Maybe it was the spreading pink hues
feathering my face
as I watched the gentle dawn
on the January sky,
as I realized each dawn of every day
is truly *not* the same.

Or maybe it was the presence larger
than myself that gathered remnants
of the past year, held them out to me
so I could see they had
more influence than I once believed.

Don't Run

Don't run
when faced with
something or someone
that seems like
an adversary

Stay with it
Try to hear it
Let the process unfold
Do not judge
Let it all be

Sooner
or maybe later
what is constricted
will lift its head
and surprise you
with how simple
the truth is

In the meantime
keep returning
to the center
surround your heart
with love
let the ugly thoughts
and harsh feelings
fade away

Don't shove them out
but never let them take over

Listen and learn

The Ice Storm

Soft moisture slides through
the frozen air, paralyzed
before it reaches the ground.
The trees feign indifference
while their lengthy boughs
accept the stony silence.

Branches soon grow heavy
and gasp with regret,
straining with the weight
of innocent hospitality.

The icy pellets terrorize
the vulnerable boughs,
the weight of their arrival
bending the strong branches
until they bow humbly to earth.

A rabbit climbs from a safe burrow,
four paws on the glazed lawn,
sniffs at the falling particles,
then slides back into the darkness,
wisely choosing the softness of home.

I, too, observe the icy raindrops
as they wrap themselves
around each piece of sidewalk,
lamppost, telephone wire, and tree,
musing to myself:

am I a prisoner of winter
or a recipient of transparent beauty?

Not So Afraid

The sparrows are spinning
warmth into the winter world.

Their delicate, clear chirps
bring with them a crisp joy,
making me not so afraid
of the howling wind.

So, too, the friends of my heart.

Melody of My Soul

At surprising times
the melody of my buoyant soul
swells to unexpected immensity,
flows through me like April leaves
humming in the breeze.

Merrily the song sways, swings
without a care, in tune
with the mysterious music
sailing through the Universe.

This unbounded harmony
tosses my well-calculated life
into tailspins of ecstasy,
lifts me high in happy pursuit
of the singing stars who know
my soul's melody by heart.

Then all within me
becomes calm
and I settle
once more
into my soul's silent glow.

A Steady Rain

All night a steady rain
fell upon the autumned earth,
moistening every dried crack
of the bony summer,
rinsing what lay tattered
and soiled in the remnants
of yesterday.

I went to sleep with the gentle rain
seeping into the edges of my dreams
and woke to its soothing melody,

each drop resuscitated my own dryness,
each wet particle from the November clouds
awakened the thirsty muse inside,
each splash of moisture softened the hard shell
containing imprisoned words, freed them
to breathe life upon the stagnant,
empty pages waiting for deliverance.

Migrating Pelicans

there they are, a thick thread
of white in the middle of the lake,
silent except for the flapping of
wide, strong wings, their large bodies
resting on the water, capturing
energy for the long trip ahead.

I look through my binoculars,
joy rising, smiling at
what I behold, the exquisiteness
of something still untamed,

longing to be close to the wildness,
inwardly beseech the pelicans to
come near, when suddenly
from the horizon a cloud of beauty
sails toward me, closer, closer,
until they are directly overhead,

so near I can easily detect
which of the black feathers
on the underside of their expansive wings
is tattered, can see
the smoothness of their wide beaks,
can hear
the windy movement of their whooshing wings
convincing me
of our existing oneness.

January Moon

the full moon slips into
the January sky
right before sunset

soft as cashmere
she pours light through
tall, black trees

winter's sunset magic
surrounds the orb of light
in water-colored hues

pale pinks and delicate blues
sweep a wide swath
across the eastern horizon

crisp air tingles my ears,
lightens my heart, and for
a brief space my steps
go easy

without the least heaviness
of grief
to hold them back

Butterfly

This morning I awoke,
felt sluggish. It was time to go out
for my morning walk.

But the warmth of day
followed by cold evening
left the walkways iced.
I decided to wait until later,
when all would be melted.

As I lay there, slowly awakening,
the image of newly hatched butterflies
came to me—how they

      hang

      there

      and wait

as the blood fills out
their fresh wings,

How they stay until
the air
dries them
enough
to fly.

This morning I was the butterfly
allowing my sleepy self
to rest, to wait, to fill with life,
to ready my wings for the day.

Contemplation

It is not we who choose
to awaken ourselves,
but God who chooses
to awaken us.

—Thomas Merton

a small frog
floating, splayed out, waiting,
all of her body in the pond
except her goggled eyes,
round buttons of attention
rising above the clear water,

a small frog,
looking, I realize, at me
while I look at her,
both curious
about the other's presence

a small frog
silently attentive,
calling me back to stillness
until I sit without purpose,

content to gaze
with an awakened
sense of wonder

Frozen Songs

the music of winter birds
waits in silent throats,
frozen in quiet crystals
of falling snow.

few warbles or chattering chirps
greet the shivering sunrise,
no luring of demure mates
as in the warm frenzy of spring.

like the birds, my silenced soul
stores her muffled songs,
resting them in the dark solitude
of icy vigil,

waiting, as we all do,
for the softening of heart
and the greening
of what has long been lost
to hibernated joy,

wistfully aware
of that graced springtime
when the voice of song rises
from creation,

when the turning of a season
opens up the silence
and frees what mutely gestated
in winter's quietude.

At Night

at night
with two pillows propped
behind me,
out of nowhere,
in the middle of turning
a page, I sigh,
realizing I am at peace,
happy and content.

I pause in my reading,
put the book down,
aware of something undefined.

what is this intangible
comfort, sweet as
springtime freesia?

I close my eyes,
breathe in
what feels like someone
tapping lovingly
on the door of my heart.

I welcome
this unseen presence,
bask in the pleasing warmth
of the unexpected visit,

sit there wrapped
in a mantle of grace,
sure now that I am enfolded
by the One Love
I am forever seeking.

Last Leaf on the Tree

The youngest of six,
five girls and one boy,
now at eighty-eight
no one left but herself.

She moves through the big house
alone with financial decisions
and all the other matters about her life,
alone with her thoughts now
no children to keep her company
no relatives nearby.

Last leaf on the tree,
that's how she describes herself,
green at eighty-eight
while the Burns family has long lain
in the family burial ground.
She hangs on with veracity,
dancing in the autumn air,
nary a sign she's about to fall
and join the others who have left her.

A sturdy woman, wise and wispy,
she talks on and on and on
full of details and descriptions,
a vibrant stream of consciousness
dancing through words
like sunlight sparkling on water.

Open, alert, ready to grow,
lover of the arts and generous to all,
she's a mentor of integrity,
a teacher of how to live beyond eighty.

On My Way From Mankato to St. Paul

The crust on my preoccupied heart
fell off
quite unexpectedly
while driving on an almost empty interstate.

The sun was sinking on the western rim,
glimmers of its gold sweeping across
mature cornfields standing silently
in their autumn robes.

A flicker of movement caught
my weary eyes.
I looked to the field in time to see
a black cloud of beauty
rising from the ripened rows of grain.

Hundreds of blackbirds swirled in
a broad circle,
spread out, lifted higher,
and then shifted back into a thick eddy
of community.

This black vortex
with its flash of movement,
there, then gone,

just enough time
to rinse my soul
of her sleepy residue.

Changing the Landscape

It doesn't take much
to change the grey drabness
of a bleak winter day,

just an inch or two of snow
soft upon the lawn and roof.

It doesn't take much
to change the stony landscape
of a rankled heart,

just a word or two of kindness
soft upon the discontent.

It doesn't take much
to change the angry mind
of a quickened hurt,

just an offering of forgiveness
soft upon the injury.

An Exile Coming Home

I've learned it is essential,
beneficial and indispensable,
to stand up to the secret power
another wields over you,

the one who's intent
on ruining your life,
who manages to convince you
that your whole self,
your entire well-being,
depends on the welfare
of the one clutching you
in the heavy grasp
of false ownership.

The only way to be freed
from deathful constraint
is to turn around and face it,

march right up to the constriction,
look it boldly in the eye
without a trace of surrender

and send it away
with your resurrected self-worth.

Bittersweet

Leaving the safe path,
the smooth road, the marked way,
I wandered far from it
on an unsure path, rutted and rough.

Halfway around a small pond
not yet frozen solid with December's cold,
bittersweet startled me, its vivid red
twining around the meandering
brambles of a grey sapling.
Forgotten was the stinging wind on my face
and the rough land under my feet.

A jubilant discovery of beauty
on an uncertain road,
with intuition as my only guide.

Easter Joy

Mary Magdalene and the other Mary
went quickly from the tomb,
fearful yet overjoyed . . .

—Matthew 28:8

Joy,
come forth in us
like the Risen One
easily slipping
from the darkened tomb.
Come with Easter gladness,
robust power
easily pushing thick stone
from a tight enclosure.

Joy,
come dance in us
like the Risen One
showing up unexpectedly.
Stir deadened grief,
startle sad eyes
into hopeful ones,
lift heavy curtains
of depression.
Emblazon your eastering
on everyone.

Joy,
come go with us
like the Risen One
into everyday places.
Gladden hearts
that have given up.
Catapult the lonely
into communities of kinship
and lift the downcast
into summersaults of hope.

The Memory of a Hand

Her feathery hand in mine,
delicate onion skin wrapped
around a hundred years of bone,
purple veins bulging
through the spotted coverlet
of age-formed blotches,
each arthritic joint rubbing
across my still-straight fingers.

But what I remember most
is not the shape, the form,
the weightlessness of that precious
hand with its long, crooked fingers.

What remains is the touch of love
formed long ago in friendship
unweathered by the extensive years,
the clasp of her soft hand in mine,
tender and warm.

Self-Doubt

Self-doubt marks my
writing experience
like feral cats
etching paw prints
in newly fallen snow.

In between the lines I write
a wild voice inserts itself
louder than any security
of past success,

goads me to eradicate
every word I've placed
on the page,
insisting the words
are worth nothing,

nothing.

Challenges me
to distrust
my belief and experience,
taunts me
to hold my words out
for others to behold.

Ah, but never mind those paw prints
in the snow,
the sun will melt all trace of them.

Self-doubt will ease away
when a stronger voice arises
telling me I was silly
to question, to listen to
the feral cats sneaking around
in the hesitations
of my mind.

Resurrection

An unknown Iowa pasture,
two black figures in the dawn,
one large, one very small,
so small as to almost not be seen,
hidden in the fresh folds
of unblemished April grass.

A mother cow gives birth,
leans down, nudges her child,
helps his wobbly legs to stand,
licks away the womb's silk
and offer the fullness of her udder.

Everyday, somewhere,
a new creation.

Everyday, somewhere,
a new life marked with splendor,
leaving behind the unwrapped linens
of an empty womb.

Memories

They say memories
can comfort the grieving.
I say good memories
can chafe the heart,
wear it bloody
with remembrance.

Part of me wants to toss
all memories away,
let the heart be freed
from what binds it
to the past.

Yet, memories do console.
How could I continue
without the gift of a face
held in my sorrowed mind,
without years of love settled
forever in my grieving bones.

Strength from memories.
Agony from memories.
Let the tension be.

Gestation

nine months of not sitting,
confined to a house,
no stooping, bending,
only standing in pain or lying flat on her back

nine months of being dependent, vulnerable,
others dressing her, caring for her,
comforting her

nine months in a body cast
have brought forth
not a child of the womb
but a child of the heart

new understanding of friendship,
of the fragility of life
and precious body movement,

deeper appreciation of walking,
driving a car, freedom to move,
and caring for oneself

nine months
of birthing herself

Rain

a few little drops
from heaven
not enough to wet
a bird feather
but welcome all the same

each tiny splash
bathes the limp faces
of scorched flowers

every morsel of moisture
soothes the dry tongue
of ragged grasses

don't complain
about the sparse falling
instead, take off your clothes
and let the few strong raindrops
rinse off your despair

Watching Each Other Age

We watch each other age,
daily changes spreading
their webby fingers
across our wrinkled features.

We notice brown splotches
and knobby, toad-like bumps
rising into life
over night.

We discover unwanted hair
springing up in undesired places,
while precious, treasured locks
swim freely down the drain.

We see illness and death
steal away those we love.
Our own swift pains and uncertain maladies
falter and sputter,
leading us to wonder when
our ending time will leap upon us.

In spite of these trailing limps
of uncertainty,
we sit and talk about much more
than weather conditions
or weighty prescription bills.

We sit and marvel at the world's exquisite beauty
which still allures us,
as does the tenderness of
all love.

We sit and wonder about the children,
children of a world gone mad
with lust for war
and greed for oil to appease
poisonous consumption.

We dream together
of a world woven with peace
and the gold of kindness.

Seven Sisters

They look quietly
with their calm black eyes,
slightly hesitant as they pause
to watch me pass by.

Seven sisters celebrating dawn,
returning to dine at sunset.
Curious, sometimes shy,
always attentive.

I sense kinship with these women
of the land, their easy glance,
their security in the seasons.

What do they speak of,
these seven does,
when no one is listening?

What do they whisper
when dawn takes a first breath?

What would they tell me
if I could lean
into their conversation?

Silent Nudge of Confidence

When the tulips
were singing their way
into budding,

when forsythia bushes
were blooming bright yellow,

the heavy, wet April snow
came with surprise,

crushing everything green,
freezing flower buds
halting warm winds
wilting fresh foliage.

But the sun returned.

The green stayed.
The snow melted.
The buds kept their strength.
Warm winds resumed.

And in my world
crushed with the weight
of violence,
frozen with the deathly cover
of war and terrorism,
there, too, I must believe
green will endure.

The buds of peace
will stand strong.

The memory of an empty tomb,
this, and the resilient earth,
give my faltering hope
a silent nudge of confidence
amid these troubled times.

Taking Back Her Life

Today she is taking back
her life
after three years
of wanting to give it away,
of hoping to cease living,

of desiring to go into the dark,
into her own death
as easily as the ripe peach
slips from the stone,

but now grief has eased.

Death no longer pursues her
and dreams of what could be
entice her with their vision.

Now she is content
with memory,
with those rare moments
when his spirit
encircles hers
with whispered presence,

when the green of spring wheat
and the sparkle of winter skies
urges her to keep embarking
on this voyage of death and rebirth.

The Best of You

I shall live on with that part of the dead
that lives forever, and I shall rekindle into life
that of the living that is now dead, until there
is nothing but life, one great life, oh God.

— Etty Hillisum

You are gone from me now,
years of grief grown paler
but still glowing steady with memory
drawing me ever toward you.

I want the best of you,
who you were in your finest clothes,
generous, forgiving, full of purest love.

Every day I ask of you
to grant just this much to me,
the best of you,
a wardrobe of goodness
wrapped in easy laughter,
an adventurous heart,
a searching soul.

How could I not yearn
daily
for what held us close,
the best of you.

(This poem was inspired by Dorothy Dee's letter about her deceased friend, Honor Keirans: "Everyday I ask Honor to give me the best of her.")

Waiting for a Return

I stand on the deck at dawn,
silent as the tall, thin cottonwoods
filling the hillside before me.

they are waiting for a return
and so am I—
the return of green,
the movement of veiled life
as it slurps through stems
and voices itself
in tree toads and crickets.

the trees wait unperplexed,
as if it matters not
how long
this snowy winter goes on.

they stand alert,
ready at the first signal to awaken,
while completely surrendered
to this February moment.

surely I can join them
in this posture of acceptance.
surely the long winter within me
can wait serenely
until I, too, leap into joy
at the first gesture of spring's ecstasy.

The Pine Grove

Finding my way in,
trying to enter
the heart of a pine grove
thick with tangled underbrush
and dry, scratchy branches.

Finally I press apart
the pine's tightly held arms,
feel the sharp resistance
of their needles
poking into my fingers.

Outside the pine grove
a fierce wind whistles
and groans
pushing its power around
with the weight of its velocity.

Once inside the protective arbor
I lay my body down in the softness
of the pine needles at its center,
amazed to feel the easy calm,
the lack of wild wind, the effortless
quiet the pine grove holds.

Much later, when I reluctantly
depart, I renew my resolution
to not let a day go by
without entering the arbor
of my morning meditation

where I part the brambly branches
of my pressured days,
and enter that same inner calmness,
that same serenity.

Winter Invitation

Winter invites me once more
to enter the cave,
to go within the within.

Outside my small cottage
wild wind swirls fresh snow
while birds cheep and chitter,
gathering at a feeder quickly emptied.

No cheeps inside my soul.
Only a persistent attempt
to honor winter's invitation
to cease my tenacious sputterings
about being stuck indoors,

to slow down the wild winds
drifting my thoughts
into a solid mass of deadness,
to get beyond the unending push
to be productive.

Hibernate. Gestate.

Wander around the inner domain
without a concern for what may,
or may not, surface.

Let myself be drawn deeper
into this winter solitude.

With Each Flying-by Year

With each flying-by year
my aging groans
a bit more loudly.
I strain to hear my heartbeat
and feel the way my muscles
stretch with resistant elasticity.

Like the thickly formed trunk
of the ancient oak
slowly falling over into soil
my youth bends toward downfall,
each new creak of bone
reminding me
of my own turtle slowness.

I see the widening creases
of my late-sixties face
mirroring the elderly oak's
thickening, ridge-lined bark

and in one long breath
I decide to let aging
take me along,
like the pale winter's sigh
in the oak's barren branches
bidding it adieu.

The Robin in January

I pause, look again.
Yes, a robin in January,
out of place, out of time,
perched on a low branch,
feathers fluffed, looking calm.

I actually speak aloud:
"What in the world are you doing
here?"

Why no southern journey?
Too late, too foolish,
too enamored with the riches
of an autumn feast?

I don't know.
But a robin in winter
seems no harbinger of spring,
no sign of hope.
Rather, a witness to courage,
or missed opportunity.

Either way, I stand amazed
and wonder what that robin
has to say to my own journey.

Watching Rain

Most of an entire day
I sat and watched the rain fall,
the hard downpour, the fullness,
the pause, the steady drip, the plop,
the softness, the gentleness.

I looked at single droplets
gather at the tip of each pine needle,
saw how the rain rinsed
the green and yellow meadow
of its dusty residue
and left the lupine shining.

I noticed the aspen leaves
slightly tremble
with each touch of moisture,
studied the fluffed fur
of the healthy chipmunk
ripping seeds
from a tall, green gentian
refreshed after the showers.

All day I observed the wetness,
the way every layer and line,
every chip and hue of color
became sharply visible,
the density and depth of bark
as rain soaked its ridges.

I studied the impermanence of clouds
that darkened, lightened,
drenched the land, receded,
leaving a thick mist behind.

I walked some in the rain, too,
but mostly gazed in silence,
a secret admirer
loving how rain can change
a landscape
and revive a deadened heart.

Blackbirds

Every September they come
with their gluttonous beaks,
feigned royalty
acting as the final authority
on who gets fed as they sit
on their newly perched throne.
Haughty, arrogant, flaunting
a you-owe-me-this attitude.
No wonder their ancestors
were baked in a pie. I've dreamed
of nasty ways to get rid of them, too.
But yesterday, the slant of the sun
fell just right on the dark feathers,
a sheen of iridescent blue
on the nape of the neck.
I tried to ignore it. Turned away.
Turned back. Exquisite, I had to admit.
Perhaps they're royalty, after all.

Easter Watch

Look for light piercing the gloom.
Receive little joys inside old troubles.
Hold on to love in bleakest of times.
Keep faith alive when filled with doubt.
Accept help from whomever it comes.
Pray in spite of strong resistance.
Laugh amid the tattered tears.

Stand at Easter's emptied tomb.
Remember what the message is.
Shake off what holds you back.
Cast your gaze inside your journey.
Meet the Risen One on the road.
Let renewed hope enter every step.

Watch how Love surprises you.

Observe the Freed One slipping
inside the story of your life.

How Many Loves Now

How many loves now
have moved across
my heart
leaving permanent marks?

How many loves now
are lost to me
by death
or fickleness
or distance?

How many loves now
press their faces
to the windowpane
of my life
and beg to come in?

How many loves now
glow inside of me
like a crackling fireplace
on a cold winter's night?

How many loves now,
how many?

I gather them all,
the well-established
the long dead
the wish-I-could-come-in
the warming-my-heart ones,

Today all of them find their place
and seem to be content.

Shabby and Awkward

Shabby and awkward,
spiritually disheveled,
I run in pursuit
of taming my untruths.

Finally I fall
into the ragged gutter
of those endless struggles,
unable to keep pushing
toward unmet goals.

Only then
does the dross disappear,
only then
does the lame get up
and walk.

When Winter Wears Long

when winter wears long
and snow swirls
around the highest window,

when the dark of night
yawns wearily through the day
and stars forget to shine,
it's a good day

to look toward the west,
catch a quick winged one
and walk along the beach,

let the sound of endless waves
wash away the sand dunes
of depression and
the sun, warm as wine,

weave a temporary cover
of winterless solitude.

let the vast Pacific shore
hide the memories
of blizzards and wind chills

while the tired heart
lifts up her face in joy.

Writing

I wait out sluggish days,
empty evenings, mulish
attempts to capture words
hiding themselves
inside the undulating sea
of my mental thesaurus,
not even remotely available
for me to scoot them
onto my fingers and
into necessary revision.

So I wait, and wait,
and wait some more
while I fumble uselessly
with worthless concoctions
until

one early dawn
the tide comes in
and the first word peeks out.

then they all follow,
and like a flock of gulls
I swoop in to snatch
the sea's latest prey.

Community

    Branches touch.

    Limbs assure one another,
    "I'm here."

    No matter how fierce the storm,
    "I'm here."

    In spite of how jagged
    and torn the branches,
    "I'm here
    beside you through the long
    turbulent nights.

    I'll reach to connect
    with you
    in the wildest of winds.

    Be assured of my presence.
    Have confidence.
    I'm here."

Home Free

the last breath
leaving the body,
the release of what
kept you here. gone.
where? I do not know,
but gone.

today the anniversary
of your departure
tugs at my tears until
they ripen and
release,

but the tears do not
last. what lingers is the memory
of leaving the hospital
and being startled into awareness,
hearing robins full of intense song
at dawn's first light,
sounding as though hundreds
were in every tree in the city,
one great symphony of joyous warbling.

At that very moment
I heard within my sorrow,
"they're singing his resurrection,"

a clear voice telling me
you were home free.

Snake Charmer

Music, that snake charmer
of my sleeping joy,
awakens currents of happiness
too long hibernated in the cave
of persistent mourning.

Music breaks through
the glazed compartment
of dull duties,
connects with the silken self
regretfully abandoned
to the graveyard of grief.

The melody of a simple song
stirs the soul,
shakes loose more sorrow
still unshed.

Only now the weeping
is tender, not discordant,
welcomed, not regretted.

And the song that awakens
the dormant joy
leaves a current of strength,
a note of hope.

Uncertainty

I doubt my words,
mistrust how they come
together, wonder if their worth
will touch anyone's heart
but my own.

I question my journey,
wonder about the travel,
prefer to stay hidden
but am unsure
what is selfish and what
is essential.

I squeeze out what
seems my last morsel
of generosity, hesitant
to give any further,
then even more is required
from those who leave
my heart emptied.

but today the sky clears
to a winter blue,
and the round moon rises
without a hint of duplicity.

inside myself
the sky also sweeps away clouds,
the moon rises clean and bright

and I am at peace
with questions that have
no answers.

Live This Day

It is time to live this day as death turns toward you
 to relish the tiny glimpses of beauty
 to look for unexpected sources of hope
 to welcome the kindness of strangers
 to breathe in some unexpected joy

It is time to linger in the moment
 to savor a simple cup of coffee
 to feel a warm ray of sunshine
 to hear the melody of a song
 to treasure the voice of a loved one

It is time to be grateful for the little things
 the gentle touch of a hand
 the water's caress in the whirlpool
 a smile on the face of a loved one
 a night when sleep holds you gently

It is time to embrace the emptiness
 to accept the body's continued weakening
 to let the naked sadness reach where it will
 to learn more from unwanted dependency
 to listen to the feelings, whatever they are

It is time to focus on where your strength lies
 to dwell with memories of happier days
 to call in your wise and loving ancestors
 to relish the true loves of your heart
 to sink into the loveliness of your being

It is time to surrender to the soul's ripening
    to watch the antics of the ego fade away
    to receive the tenderness of the Divine
    to sit quietly and embrace the silence
    to open your heart to how love calls

It is time for dying, one day at a time
It is time to accept the arduous, unknown
    journey
It is time to live as serenely as you can
It is time

Someday

Someday I will sail
those wings

Someday I will soar
with eagerness

Someday I will release
all deadness

Someday I will
tuck my heart
into the clear sky of freedom
and never, ever
look back

Index of Titles and First Lines